A+ Alphabet Books

Dogs ABC

An Alphabet Book

by B. A. Hoena

Consulting Editor: Gail Saunders-Smith, PhD

Capstone
press

Mankato, Minnesota

A is for affection.

People give their dogs affection.
They hug them. They pet them.
Dogs need lots of love and attention.

B is for bone.

Dogs chew and chomp on bones.
Rawhide bones help dogs' teeth
stay healthy and clean.

C is for catch.

A dog doesn't need a glove to play catch.
Throw a Frisbee or a ball, and the dog
will catch it in her mouth.

D is for doghouse.

A dog needs a place to stay warm when it's cold. He needs a place to stay dry when it's raining outside. A dog needs a house, a doghouse.

E is for ears.

What's that you hear? Dog ears can be floppy. Dog ears can be pointy. Dog ears can be big or small, furry or fluffy.

F is for fetch.

Throw a stick, and a dog will run
to fetch it for you. If you throw
the stick some more, she'll go get it
again and again and again.

G is for guide dog.

Guide dogs see for people who can't see. They let their owners know when to stop and when to go.

H is for hunting dog.

Hunting dogs sniff the air. When they point their noses at a clump of brush, they're saying, "Birds are hiding over there."

I is for itch.

Not all itches are easy to reach. A dog uses his paws and claws to scratch.

J is for jump.

Some dog owners train their dogs to jump. Dogs jump over fences as they race through obstacle courses.

K is for kiss.

Puppies kiss with a nudge of their noses or a slurp of their tongues. Puppies kiss to show their love. **SMOOCH!**

L is for leash.

A dog brings his leash to say, "Lets go for a walk." He'll tug and pull with all his might, so you better hold on tight!

M is for mother.

A mother dog gives her puppies lots of puppy love. She feeds her puppies and keeps them safe.

N is for nose.

A dog smells the air with her nose.
"What was here?" she wants to know.
SNIFF. SNIFF.

O is for obey.

"Stay," the owner says, and the dog obeys.
A well-behaved dog learns to listen
to his owner.

P is for play.

Puppies love to play. They wrestle.
They run. They chase after feet
and lick people's faces.

Q is for quick.

Race dogs are quick as they zip around the track. Faster and faster they run, trying to win the race. **ZOOOOOOM!**

R is for ride.

Dogs enjoy going for rides.
They'll hop into cars or get
in wagons. Dogs are curious
to learn about new places.

S is for sick.

Dogs get sick just like people do. They sneeze and sniffle. When a dog feels sick, she may not want to play with you.

T is for tag.

"What's my name? Where do I live? My tag will tell you what you want to know. If I'm lost, my tag will help you call my home."

ZAK
555-1234

U is for ugly.

Some dogs are ugly. Some dogs are wrinkly or fuzzy, thin or pudgy, but dog owners don't care. They love their dogs just as they are.

V is for veterinarian.

Veterinarians are doctors who care for animals. Vets give dogs checkups and help them stay healthy. Vets also give dogs shots. **OUCH!**

W is for wag.

What does a wagging tail mean? Dogs wag
their tails to say, "Hello! Wanna play?"

X is for excited.

Dogs get excited when they see something yummy. They'll stand up and beg. **ARF! ARF!**

Y is for yowl.

A dog yowls because he's at home and all alone. He misses his owner. **AHROOOOO!**

Z is for zzzzz.

Puppies get tired after playing all day, so it's time for bed. They're falling asleep. Good night, puppies. **ZZZZZ.**

Fun Facts about Dogs

Boxers are named after the way in which they play. When boxers play with other dogs, they stand on their hind legs and bat at the other dogs with their front paws. Boxers look like they are trying to "box" when they play.

At least one-third of U.S. dog owners talk to their dogs on the phone. Many dog owners leave messages on their answering machines so their dogs can hear their voices.

Most dogs understand between 35 and 45 spoken words.

Dogs see differently than people do. Colors don't look as bright to dogs as they do to people.

When dogs yawn, it shows that they feel safe and comfortable.

Dogs sweat through the pads on their paws. They also pant to cool off their bodies.

More than 1 million stray dogs live in the New York City area. This number is more than the number of people who live in the state of South Dakota.

Glossary

affection (uh-FEK-shuhn)—a great liking for someone or something

checkup (CHEK-uhp)—a medical examination to make sure a dog is healthy

curious (KYUR-ee-uhss)—excited to find out about something new

obstacle course (OB-stuh-kuhl KORSS)—a type of racetrack with fences and other obstacles that a dog must leap over or run through

rawhide (RAW-hide)—the skin of a cow or other animal before it has been made into leather; dogs chew on bones that are made out of rawhide.

veterinarian (vet-ur-uh-NER-ee-uhn)—a doctor who treats sick or injured animals; veterinarians also check animals to make sure they are healthy.

Read More

Ajmera, Maya, and Alex Fisher. *A Kid's Best Friend.* It's a Kid's World. Watertown, Mass.: Shakti for Children/Charlesbridge, 2002.

Dog Artlist Collection. *The Dog from Arf! Arf! to Zzzzzz.* New York: HarperCollins, 2004.

Khu, Jannell. *Dogs.* My World of Animals. New York: PowerKids Press, 2004.

Internet Sites

FactHound offers a safe, fun way to find Internet sites related to this book. All of the sites on FactHound have been researched by our staff.

Here's how:
1. Visit *www.facthound.com*
2. Type in this special code **0736826068** for age-appropriate sites. Or enter a search word related to this book for a more general search.
3. Click on the **Fetch It** button.

FactHound will fetch the best sites for you!

Index

A+ Books are published by Capstone Press
151 Good Counsel Drive, P.O. Box 669, Mankato, Minnesota 56002
www.capstonepress.com

1 2 3 4 5 6 09 08 07 06 05 04

Library of Congress Cataloging-in-Publication Data
Hoena, B. A.
  Dogs ABC: an alphabet book / by B. A. Hoena.
  p. cm.—(A+ alphabet books.)
  Includes bibliographical references (p. 31) and index.
  ISBN 0-7368-2606-8 (hardcover)
  1. Dogs—Juvenile literature. 2. English language—Alphabet—Juvenile literature. [1. Dogs.
2. Alphabet.] I. Title. II. Alphabet (Mankato, Minn.) III. Series.
SF426.5.H58 2004
428.1'3—dc22   2003027799

Summary: Introduces dogs through photographs and brief text that uses one word relating to
  dogs for each letter of the alphabet.

Credits
Amanda Doering and June Preszler, editors; Heather Kindseth, designer; Kelly Garvin,
  photo researcher; Eric Kudalis, product planning editor

Photo Credits
Brand X Pictures, 14; Brand X Pictures/G. K. & Vikki Hart, 20, 29 (left); Bruce Coleman Inc./Jane
Burton, 17; Capstone Press/Gary Sundermeyer, 5, 15, 16, 21; Corbis/Charles Mann, 3; Corbis/Jim
Craigmyle, 8; Corbis/Jim Zuckerman, 27; Corbis/Larry Williams, 23; Corbis/Rick Gomez, 2;
Corbis/Tom Brakefield, 9; Creatas/Picture Quest, 12; Digital Vision, 6, 25; Getty Images,
Inc./PhotoDisc Blue, cover; Heather Kinseth, 1; Index Stock Imagery/Peter Adams, 18; Kent &
Donna Dannen, 10; Mark Raycroft, 7; Mira/Karen Stewart, 11; Nancy M. McCallum, 19;
PhotoDisc Inc., 28 (right, phone); PhotoDisc Inc./Jules Frazier, 28 (left); Pix'n Pages/2004 C.
Gutherie, 4; Ron Kimball, 13; Stockbyte, 22, 24, 26, 28 (right, dog), 29 (right)

Note to Parents, Teachers, and Librarians
Dogs ABC: An Alphabet Book uses colorful photographs and a nonfiction format to
introduce children to characteristics about dogs while building a mastery of the
alphabet. This book is designed to be read independently by an early reader or to be
read aloud to a pre-reader. The images help early readers and listeners understand the
text and concepts discussed. The book encourages further learning by including the
following sections: Fun Facts about Dogs, Glossary, Read More, Internet Sites, and
Index. Early readers may need assistance using these features.